Hello guys today I am going to talk about an interesting module known as goal setting and time management. Well, before we even begin to talk about this module, I would want you to ask yourself these three questions, introspect and ask yourself these three questions.

One, do you have any goals in life? Two? Have you ever tried to think about or write about these goals? And three, have you ever reviewed these goals on a weekly, monthly or a yearly time period? Well, if you have answered no to each of these questions, this is for you would really be keen to watch out for.

So let's get started. Today we are going to talk about effective guidelines about what exactly is goal, how to set goals and how to make a really wonderful action plan for yourself to achieve your dreams and your goals.

The agenda today is going to be very specifically on goal setting. we will understand and define goals and goal setting. Why don't most of the people set goals? We will throw a lot of light on this understanding the nuances of effective goal setting SMART goals Now this acronym called SMART goals is something we will talk a lot in detail about.

Each of this stands for a particular reason why goals fail, so the reasons why goals fail in life, guidelines for setting goals and different types of goals. These are all the sub modules of goal setting that we will cover today. Well, if I have to define what exactly is a goal, a dictionary definition of goals says, goal is a point marking the end of a race, an object of effort or an ambition.

It's like a final destination which you want to achieve and really go to goal setting is defined as the process of deciding what you want to do in life and also devising a plan to achieve what you want to achieve. Goal setting my friends is a very, very powerful tool. It will help you give a direction to your life. And once you have a direction in your life, life becomes even more enjoyable to live.

Let's understand the reasons why a lot of people don't set goals. Well, there is a lot of research done on this particular reason. And some of these reasons are pessimistic attitudes. Well, a lot of people think way negatively about goals and they feel that why do we really have to set goals so they feel it's a little negative to set goals for themselves? Fear of failure.

This is a reason why a lot of people fear that they will have a failure if they don't set goals and that's the reason they don't really go on the path of goal setting because they fear failure. Ignorance about the importance of goals.

They don't really know what is the importance of goal setting and hence they do Not really set goals, a lack of knowledge about goal setting, they don't really know where to start, how to go about this entire process of goal setting.

And they feel it's not rocket science to really set goals and hence, because of which they forget or rather fail to set goals.

A lot of people lack ambition. Now, by lacking ambition, I'm really trying to say that people have comfort in the comfortable zone. And they don't want to challenge themselves. They don't have any great ambitions to achieve in life, and hence they are okay staying the way they are. So lack of ambition is also a reason why people don't set goals. Low self esteem, they don't think really highly about themselves, and that's why they don't set goals.

And last but not the least, they fear having a rejection. And rejection, my dear friends can be a very powerful way of not setting goals. So my friends, these are all the reasons why people don't set goals and let's understand that are all there in our mind, we need to overcome our emotions, we need to overcome all these fears to really try and achieve goals for ourselves.

Well, if you might have even set goals, goals tend to fail.

The reason why goals fail is probably you have not written down the goals. Goals, if they are not written they are mere words. Hence, goals need to be written down and they need to be written down in the present tense. Not having any rewards for yourself also may be a reason why goals fail, not realistic. You may set very unachievable or unrealistic goals for yourself.

Well, that my friends can also lead to a failure of setting these goals. Your goals may keep changing, you might have one goal one day and after 10 days you might change the goal to one other thing, while the mind and the brain gets confused in this regard enhances can be a failure of setting goals. no accountability, no ownership. If you don't set goals and take accountability and ownership for them, it leads to a failure of goals.

Well, what I'm trying to really say here is set goals for yourself, not for your parents, not for your bosses, your managers, not for your friends or siblings, set goals for yourself, because only then you will have accountability and ownership for the same. No time lines. This can also be one of the major reasons why goals fail. If you do not have a time guideline or a time deadline to achieve these goals, you will really not know when you will achieve it.

Hence, my friends these are the reasons why we need to really keep sure that we are not able to achieve these goals and failure of these goals. Why do we really need to set goals? What are the benefits of setting goals? Let's take a look at this Well, if you set goals you take control and charge of your life, you know the direction of your life where it's going. And when you know where you want to go, you are setting yourself in the right direction so you have control over your life.

You focus on the more important things and hence waste, not waste time under unnecessary things. You will make good decisions if you have set goals, you will definitely make smarter and more correct decisions in life. You can finish off the task very efficiently. If you have set goals for yourself.

You will definitely be very very confident if you have set goals. And last but not the least, you are one step closer to success. And that might be your friends is the reason why we want to set goals. Well if we know that there are so many benefits of setting goals. Why don't we set goals? This is something I would really want you to ask yourself.

Now there are different types of goals. I would rather be divided into two categories by saying there are personal goals and there are professional goals. We want most of you to really focus on these two different aspects in a different way. You should always bifurcate yourself your goals into personal goals and your professional goals.

There are three types under these two categories. You have short term goals, mid term goals and long term goals. Well, short term goals are nothing but having goals which are set for one to two years from now. Your mid term or medium term goals are from three to five years from now, and your long term goals are beyond five years.

Well, if you want to really be effective in goal setting, set goals, short term, midterm and long term write down all of these. There are two steps for goal setting. Please do not think that goal setting is a very big process. And it really involves a lot of work. Yes, it does involve a lot of work, but it is no rocket science, it is easy to do. So let's understand two steps of setting goals.

The first part of setting a goal is you need to decide what you want to do. This is very important, you need to know where you want to go in life. And once you know that you need to work at accomplishing an action plan to take you forward towards that goal.

So two step deciding what you want to do. And once you know that devising an action plan to get there. Well, for most of the people, it is the second part of the step of goal setting which is problematic or difficult for them. We have this to make it very easy for you.

Let's see what they are. Well, goal setting is important because of different reasons and we need to set our goal statement for the same goal sheet will help us to have motivating goals and once we are motivated, we will definitely achieve our goals. It helps us to set SMART goals which we will cover in a little while from now. It helps to have goals in writing. As I said before, goals which are not written are mere words. It's just nothing but dreams and needs. Goals need to be written down.

Making an action plan is very important to a goal setting process. Sticking with it is very important. Do not write a goal and then leave it you need to stick with it. And last but not least, you need to read it every single day of your life.

Have your goal in front of you always and look at it morning and night or wherever during the day you can. Make sure you read your goals. The more you read your goals, the more it helps to stick in the brain. Identifying your goals is very important. You need to know what your goals are for this particular part of the process.

In terms of knowing what your goals are. I would want each of you to sit separately with yourself, no technology, no kind of phones or laptops or iPads, no music, nothing even no family members around you seclude yourself in one corner of your home or wherever outside you find the peace time, spend about 30 to one minute of your this time and try and understand and write down what your goals are in life.

Try and write it down and make sure that you go through it again and again. Question yourself and identify what your goals are.

Your goal statement needs to have these three questions which you need to ask yourself and that's very, very essential. Ask yourself these three questions. First, what do you want to achieve? really ask yourself what you want to achieve? Why do you want to achieve it? There has to be a reason behind everything. Your mind needs reasons.

So always ask yourself why do you really want to achieve that? a particular thing. And thirdly, how will you achieve it? Once you have answered all these three questions, your goal statement is ready to be made. And my dear friends, it's very important that you do not miss out on any of these questions because anything which you do not answer, you will not be able to complete this entire goal setting procedure.

Now we're coming into our most important module of this particular section on goal setting. How to Set SMART goals. Firstly, let's understand what is the acronym smart standing for S stands for specific. M stands for being measurable, a is achievable, R is realistic and T is timely.

Well if you make a goal and if it is not a SMART goal, it is not worth wasting your time and energy on your goal needs to be smart and now we are getting into how to make it a SMART goal as well. Stands for, as I mentioned before, specific, your goal needs to be specific and not general. For it to be specific, you need to ask yourself certain questions like, who, what, where, when, and why. I'm just going to share an example with you. If you want to be rich, and you say something like this to yourself, I want to be rich.

Is this a SMART goal? Not really, because it's a general statement. I want to be rich. The moment you specify it by how much you want to be rich, when you want to be rich, and how will you be rich is when you make it a SMART goal. So answering all these questions makes your goal specific.

These questions are important to answer and hence only then will your goal Be specific. coming to our next terminology, measurable, your goal needs to be measured by asking how much or how many how will I know when it is accomplished? So if I'm quoting the same example as I did last time, I want to be rich, well, how much do you want to be rich by and how will you know when you have achieved that? So, making it more measurable by saying something like I want to be rich by having $30 million in my account, well, now you have measured it and that is what is known as measurable goals.

The third thing is achievable. Now, my dear friends, it's very important to have goals which are not very unrealistic or unattainable or unachievable. Hence, because of which you might be demotivated if you do not achieve it. So your goals need to be achievable. It has to be doable, it's something that you should be knowing and doable is what is important.

It must be action oriented, and it must be within reach. I would just like to specify that you cannot really say something like this. I want to have a hundred billion dollars in my account tomorrow. When Is it achievable? Not really unless you hit a lottery. Well, that's my idea, my friend is purely based on luck. Hence, what I'm trying to really say here is to have goals which are achievable and not something which is beyond your reach. Otherwise you get demotivated, and that's not good.

Coming to our next acronym, R stands for realistic. Your goal needs to be realistic, it should be real and relevant to your current situation. It's something that you want to achieve and it has to be relevant to what your current situation is. If it is not relevant to your current situation.

It is not realistic, and hence, it's not a SMART goal. People must believe that it is realistic. If you want to achieve an epitome of success. Your SMART goals have to be relevant to what you're doing. You might be studying in a particular section or might become pursuing arts or commerce. But if you are setting a goal which is of a different field altogether, it is not a realistic goal.

The last part of our SMART goal stands for t which is time bound, your goals need to have a specific time frame within which you will complete that goal.

Example, I want to be rich by $30 million in the year 2019, for example, now that is something which is time bound because you have put a time frame to it, making it even more specific by saying 21st March 2019 is when I want to have $30 million in my account. Well, you have made it so specifically time bound that your brain starts working around that.

So, time boundaries, you should have an established time frame. That should be realistic and everyone should be aware of your time frame. So try and make it as public and talk to people about it. That's great for your SMART goals as well. I would like to share certain facts about goal setting with you.

Let's understand what these Facts are specific, realistic goals always work best. So don't have general goals, have specific and realistic goals they really work. It takes time for a change to become an established habit. Well, when you have started this process of goal setting, you need to make certain changes in your attitude and behavior. And for this to become an established habit will take a little time. But my dear friends, do not lose your patience over here.

Repeating our goals makes it stick so start making it a habit to repeat your goals and make it stick. Pleasing other people doesn't always work. You don't have to please anyone. Be true to yourself and define your goals. roadblocks doesn't always mean failure. Well, when you are on your path to achieving your goals, you will meet a lot of obstacles in your way and a lot of hindrances which might come in your way.

Have patience and try to overcome these roadblocks which We'll come on your way. Certain quotations to motivate you to set your goals let's look at them. Without goals and a plan to reach them. You are like a ship that has set sail, but with no destination. If you can dream it, you can do it. So dream Your Goals are your road maps that guide you and show you what is possible.

And lastly, a dream is just a dream. But a goal is a dream with a plan and a deadline. Well, my dear friends, I do hope these quotations have motivated you, encouraged you and really excited you to set your goals. I'd like to conclude this goal setting by urging you to identify your goals. Make your action plan and achieve your goals. Have a vision in life, have a mission in life. Keep it always in front of you, which will really make you achieve your goals with a lot of energy and enthusiasm. Never lose. That.

Next interesting module and one of my personal favorites is called time management. Well, if you want to be a world class leader, have a good work life balance and generally want to be successful in your career and in your life. This is a module that you need to pay a lot of attention on. Well, the agenda today is what we're going to be covering in this module of time management. Some of the sub topics are effective time management, learning how to plan and prioritize your day properly.

Importance of time logs and to do lists and how they help you manage your time better Identifying our time wasters and time robbers. Well, it's important to know where exactly we are wasting our time because unless we don't know that we are not going to be able to manage your time properly. So we will understand the Pareto principle of 80 by 20. This is a very important concept which was coined by Mr. Eason hobo, and he has explained to us how this Pareto principle of 80 by 20 works. Well, we are also going to talk about the urgent and important matrix. This interesting concept was coined by Mr. Steven Covey, and he has made us understand the importance between urgent and important tasks being busy versus being productive.

So, these are what we are going to cover in our module. Let's get started. Well, everyone gets 24 hours in a day, nobody gets more and nobody gets less. So, why is it that some people are always struggling to manage their time, are always running pillar to post and always trying to squeeze in so much in their 24 hours, still having no time for themselves? At the end of the day, these people complain.

I don't have time on the other set. We have Another group of people who are able to manage all their time very, very properly, they are able to prioritize, they are able to plan and they are able to accomplish everything in a day's time. At the end of the day, they have a lot of time for themselves and are always productive.

The difference between these two sets of people is that the latter set of people are always the kind of people who have learned the technique of time management. And that is the reason why we having this on time management to help us become productive and be good at our work. Why do we need time management? Well, there are a lot of benefits associated with being able to manage your time properly.

And once we know what these benefits are, we are definitely going to strive to be better with our time management. So let's understand what these benefits of time management are. The most important benefit is time management helps you to save time. Well Time is money in today's day. Time lost will never come back again will it? So, time saved is equal to money on.

Time management helps you to reduce stress. We are so stressed out in today's life. Why? Because we squeeze in too much into our day without realizing whether we are able to manage our time to all these different tasks that we have squeezed in. So it helps you to stress free yourself.

Time management helps us to function effectively as a constructive and productive worker at our workplace. It helps to increase our work output. It helps us have more control over our job responsibility. So we are actually able to really function well and be a productive team member with our employees.

It helps you to prioritize. It helps us to plan our tasks better, know what to do first and know what to do last. So scheduling our priorities is something that will be a great benefit of time management. It helps us to get more done in less time. And isn't that what we all strive for, we all have so much to do. And so little time, it helps you to do less in an amount of time. It tells us to give good quality of work. And we all should strive for quality work rather than just finishing off our tasks and doing more multiple tasks.

Quantity is not so good. But quality is always better, it helps us to discipline ourselves. And last, but not the least it helps you to make sure that you deliver what is promised. These are some of the benefits of time management. And I'm sure listening to all this, you would definitely want to learn how to save time, how to manage your time.

Now there is a very interesting concept. A lot of people feel that they're busy, and they're also productive. Well busy does not mean being productive. Busy and productive are two different things. You might say I'm very busy doing something. But when someone asks you what are you busy doing? That is a question mark on your face and you're really not sure what are you busy doing? But you tend to want to be busy. So what is the difference between being busy and being productive? Let's understand that a little in detail being busy.

There are people who have multiple priorities, they will have numerous priorities for themselves, whereas productive people on the other hand, they only focus on few priorities. They would rather focus on a lesson number of things, rather than filling their days with too many things. Busy people always respond with a yes they will never say no for a task or an activity. Whereas productive people on the other hand, always think twice before they say yes to somebody.

Busy people when they are working, they will keep all the doors opened, so anybody can disturb them and interrupt them, which is not a good thing. On the other hand, productive people when they are at work, they will close the Doors they will never let you interrupt them or make them you know, understand what that is, keep talking about how busy they are busy people always keep on hopping. I'm very busy doing this and that. Well, on the other hand, productive people.

They don't go on harping about how busy they are. They let the results speak for themselves. And isn't that always a better option? They see people are multitaskers they will do numerous amount of things on lots of things. At one point of time, they will multitask whereas productive people will only concentrate on one important task or one important goal.

Now let's understand according to research our mind if it is focused on too many things at the same time, you will not deliver quality work in any of those tasks because your mind is in different tasks. However, if you focus on one particular task or Goal, unable to finish that, that's always a much better option. So we should always strive to do this rather than this. Well busy people, they always ask for advice. On the other hand, productive people, they take real actions and they get the job done. Rather than only asking people for advice, they do that but at the same time they do the work.

They work on their actions, rather than only talking to people about advice and suggestions. So what we're trying to say in this particular slide is always strive to be productive, rather than only being busy. Now one of the very important ways of, you know, managing our time is being able to create something which is known as a productivity journal.

Now, a productive journal is nothing but a time log of your day to day activities, what you do in your entire day's time, right from the time you get up to the time you retire to bed at night. So let's understand the productive journal, we should have two journals, one for personal and one for professional, it's important to bifurcate these two journals. Always label it with the time, the time of the day, the date and your name on the journal.

Prioritize your first three tasks, it's very important to jot down or to write down what you want to accomplish your first three priorities of your day. It's important to use your productive journal every day, don't just use it once and then let go of it for the next 15 days and then open your journal again. It's something that I would want you to work on every single day of your life. And that's the crux of managing your time properly.

Well, how do you maximize using your productivity journal? It's important to plan the night before. Now the reason why I say plan the night before is because when you sleep at night, your subconscious mind is the most alert at that point of time and Whatever you feed into the mind at that time, stays with you till the morning hours.

Hence it's very important. Plan your task the night before, rather than doing it after getting up in the morning. prioritize your task. When we talk about prioritizing. What I'm really trying to say is that I understand what tasks need to be done first and what time needs to be done second, third, and so on and so forth.

Prioritizing your task is very important and we will throw a lot of light on it later on in the module. Cross off completed tasks, there is nothing more accomplished or motivating then putting a tick mark in your productive journal saying that you have finished this task. It gives you mental satisfaction.

And yes, there is a hormone which gets released whenever you feel motivated and proud and that's important. carry over unfinished tasks. If for some reason you have not been able to complete a particular task in a day, it's okay does not matter. You can get Over the next day. This is again a very important way of managing your time better having to do a list. Now to do list is a concept which most of us really know about but haven't really practiced. It is a question I would want you to ask yourself to do Lists are very important to make sure that all your tasks get captured, completed within a specific point of time in your day.

The reason why we say to do lists is important is because you are able to write down everything and know what all other things you need to do in a day. There is a step by step approach and I would really want you to follow this whenever you are making a to do list. So let's understand what are these four steps which will help us make a to-do list. Step one, capture everything you need to do.

However small or big. The task doesn't matter. You capture everything on a piece of paper, writing down everything that needs to be done. Small Big doesn't matter. The second step is to follow ABC method of priority. Now when I say follow ABC method, what I'm really trying to say is all those tasks which you feel are most important, just write a in front of them, which you feel are less important right b in front of them. And whatever you feel is the least important right c in front of them. This way you have to prioritize your task which you have written down for yourself.

Step three is you need to write down how long does each and every step take. Now, what I would want you to do is try to understand that each task needs some time that you need to give to that particular task.

So what is the time you want to give to that you need to write in front of that. It's going to take an hour's time, half an hour's time, two hours time, you need to write that down. The fourth step is as I mentioned earlier, take when the task is done. It is very motivating to know that you have accomplished So much in a day, it's motivating, isn't it?

This is again, a very important way of managing your time, chunk, block and tackle. Now when we are faced with a very huge project that we need to do, it is very overwhelming for us. It is something that we get scared of or have afraid of fewer apprehensions. Such a big task, how am I going to do it? Well, you have something which is known as chunk block and tackle.

This will help you manage your overwhelming task and get it done. How do we need to do? We need to break down the project if it's a big project, break it down into smaller manageable tasks that will help you get started. Second, set time for a specific task. Those small tasks that you have, you know, kind of motivated down for yourself.

Try to have a set amount of time that you will take to complete Each task, avoid interruptions. When you have blocked or rather chunks of small small pieces of a task, always have a small set of time that you will assign aside to each task. And also, trying not to get interrupted during that when you're focused on something, Please give your hundred percent to it.

Avoid phone calls, avoid emails or white technology, try to just be focused on that one task and tackle one task at a time. As I mentioned before, don't multitask. If you're focused on one task, it gets completed much better. Next, we are going to talk about how to prioritize your time. Well, time management is not only about learning how to manage time, it's about learning how to manage yourself in relation to time and this particular concept has very beautifully been shared with us by Mr. Easton. Whoa.

Mr. Easton Hogan has told us that it is important to answer. This time how to prioritize your time with something which is known as an urgent, important matrix. Let's understand what is an urgent, important matrix. Well, what is urgent and what is important? Is there a difference between these two terms or are they similar?

Well, if you don't do the important task, they become urgent and that's something that we want to avoid. We want to avoid being in an urgent zone. So let's start doing the important tasks before they become urgent.

Here we are going to talk about four quadrants. Quadrant one which is urgent and important. Quadrant two which is important but not very urgent. Quadrant three which is not even urgent and not important and quadrant four, which is urgent but not important. Let's understand a little in detail about what these four quadrants are now. The first quadrant urgent and important meaning you are always running to manage your pressing problems. It's a crisis situation you're running for projects meetings, trying to accomplish everything in a day and that is when you are in this quadrant urgently and very important for you.

The second quadrant is important but not urgent. Now, what do we mean by important but not urgent, these are certain tasks which you need to make sure you do in time before they become urgent. So, some things like preparation, prevention, value clarification, planning your life, your goals, your vision, relationship building spending, quality time with your family members going also vacations, recreations etc.

These are not very important things, but yes, they are important if you give yourself the time to be in the zone. Quadrant two is very, very essential and important to be in quadrant three is not important but it is urgent for some people, why are you at your desk working, you might get some interruptions, some important meals to send some important phone call which comes in your way.

Well, these are things that we want to avoid, why because they are urgent for some other people. But you start wasting your time in this quadrant because you give a lot of attention to these pressing problems, meetings, some or the other report which needs to be sent etc. So try to avoid being in this quadrant.

Quadrant number four is not even urgent and not important. One of the most important activities which I would say in today's time is social media. We are so busy with our WhatsApp with our Facebook, Instagram, Twitter, etc. We spend so much time on these activities that half of our day is completely filled with these and then we don't have time for our urgent and important tasks.

So any junk mail. Some phone calls are time wasters and escape activities are really not helping us much manage our time. When we are in this particular zone, we are only wasting our important time of the day by filling it with these activities. Now, out of all these four quadrants, if you really want to manage your time we'll be in quadrant number two, which is important but not urgent.

Once we start being in quadrant two, we will learn how to manage our life and our time much better. We are next going to talk about our Pareto principle, which is the 80 by 20 rule. Mr. Pareto came up with this particular concept, which is known as Pareto principle, way back in the 1900s. Well, what he's really trying to say is focus on 20% of your actions which will reap 80% of the results.

The Pareto principle says put your efforts where they will make the most difference. Most of us try to accomplish too much in a day, rather accomplish the important things in a day, which only call for 20% of those activities, which will actually help you to reap a lot of benefit, which is 80%. Well, even if you look back into times back, people who actually own 20% of the land make 80% of the money. So try and understand to focus on only those tasks which are only 20% important but will actually give you 80% of the result.

Benefits of 80-20 Well, it helps you to identify the most important task or problems which you need to take care of. Secondly, it helps you to concentrate on your strength. Now we all know what our strengths and weaknesses are. So it helps you to concentrate on those activities which you enjoy doing and which you love to do. So concentrate on your strengths.

It helps you in undivided focus. Now when you know what you have to do, you try to focus your attention, your hundred percent attention on that activity. And lastly, you use the tools which are most needed resources like time, energy, money, everything is needed for this particular 20% of your actions.

So it helps you in that these are certain benefits of the 80 by 20 tool, I would really strongly recommend starting using the Pareto principle as well as the urgent important matrix if you want to manage your time a little better. Well, what we're going to cover now is one of the most fundamentals of time management, which is learning how to tackle procrastination.

Now procrastination means not being wanting to complete a particular task, setting it off for some other time, date, month, or you're saying that you want to complete the more pleasurable tasks rather than the unpleasurable task, wanting to do the less important or urgent things rather than the urgent and important things.

So human beings by nature are very lazy and careless and they don't want to do things at that particular time. How do we tackle procrastination is something which will help you really manage your time and life better? Well, we have certain tips and tricks to share with you, which will help you tackle procrastination.

There are nine ways in which you can actually overcome this habit of procrastination. And let's understand what these nine ways are. The first one is deleted. Well, if you feel a task is just getting carried over again and again, another day, another time another week, it's better to delete that task because it is not meant to be you're not meant to do that task, rather better deleted from your list.

The second way is delegate. Now delegation is a very important way of managing your time, delegate that particular task to somebody who has the time and resources and the intelligence to do that particular task. delegation works very, very well if you want to be a successful leader. The third way is Do it, just do the task, finish it off. Rather than thinking about planning, finish it off and just do it.

The next way is to follow something which is known as a 15 minute rule. Now what this means is, when you have a task in hand, Think it over in your mind, if you are able to complete it within 15 minutes, just complete it that very time, do not delay it or do not procrastinate it just within 15 minutes, finish it off.

The next thing is chop it up. Well, as we mentioned before, if there is an overwhelming big project, which you need to do, and you're really wondering, where do I start from? Well chop it up into smaller bits and pieces, and that's where you will be able to manage doing this particular task.

Next is asking for advice. A lot of times we procrastinate a particular task or work because we don't have the expert knowledge of how do we go about doing it. So ask for advice. Do a risk ask seniors or ask your leaders who will help you give you that recommended advice which will help you do that task rather than procrastinated.

The next way of dealing with procrastination is have clear set deadlines. Most of our tasks gets procrastinated because we have not assigned a clear deadline. So assign a deadline to your task because that will help you overcome this procrastination. The next one is rewarding yourself. Well, nothing is more motivating than rewarding yourself.

Give yourself a nice pat on your back saying that you Well, you have accomplished this particular thing. It's motivating and it's really good for your self esteem and self confidence. So next time you finish off a task, reward yourself. The next way is to remove distractions. When you are focusing on a very important and urgent task for yourself. There might be a lot of interruptions, distractions, please It's a request to avoid these distractions just focus on your work.

Well, by following these nine ways of overcoming procrastination, you are one step closer to managing your time, much better. Now, when we talk about time management, there are definitely going to be some barriers, some obstacles, which will not let you manage your time. Well, what are these obstacles and barriers? Let's understand, not having clear objectives.

So unclear objectives really lead to lack or less of time management because you don't know where to get started. You don't know what to do or what not to do. So having clear directions have clear objectives, why you want to do that particular task. The next is being disorganized.

Nothing can be more irritating and annoying than being disorganized. Wherever you are, whether at work or at your home, always have your table and your area organized.

Well. If you're organized, you're able to get more done in less than number of time. Lack of planning If you do not plan, you will never be able to schedule your task properly.

So always have good planning and prioritization. Avoid disruptions and interruptions. That's one of the major ways of effective time management when you are able to avoid any kind of interruption in your day. Focus on your task that's essential and important.

The next part of our module on time management is understanding what are our time wasters? We waste so much time within our 24 hours, you will not believe it, but yes, it is true. We waste 80% of our day on activities which are not really productive and taking us towards where we want to be. Well, this is something which we are going to cover on time management, understanding our time wasters. So avoiding interruptions and distractions.

Poor planning, not able to plan well, perfectionism. expecting too much to perfectness try to do everything yourself, and that's where we falter because we are not able to identify where to delegate the task or where not to delegate the task. taking on too many responsibilities, taking on too much on yourself, which is not a great thing to do.

Crisis Management. Yes, too much of socializing. We tend to socialize too much during our day. Try to do too many things, meet too many people spend too much time with our friends and family, which might not really help you solve the problem of time management, not valuing your own time.

If you don't value our time, nobody else will value your time and lack of skills. Well, these are certain areas or certain problems which will creep up which are your time wasters and time robbers. Once we know how to deal with all of these things, we are one step closer to managing our time better.

Well, I would like to only conclude by saying that time is equal to money, time spent or time lost, we'll never come back again. Learn how to prioritize, learn how to schedule your priorities, learn how to manage your time better. If you want to be a world class leader if you want to be successful in your life, manage your time well.

Thank you all for reading. And I hope you will practice all that you have learned here. Thank you and have a wonderful day.